Neptune's Daughters

Neptune's Daughters

Jenny Johnson

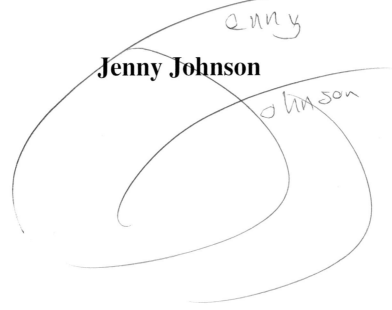

enny

ohnson

www.jennyjohnsondancepoet.net

Feedback Welcomed

Date of Publication
1999

Published by
Expansions Unlimited
Nottingham

Printed by
ProPrint
Riverside Cottage
Great North Road
Stibbington
Peterborough PE8 6LR

ISBN: 1 900410 05 2

Photograph (Back Cover) by Marilyn Hyde
Cover Illustration by Lin-Marie Foster

CONTENTS

NEPTUNE'S DAUGHTERS

SECONDS

SAPPHO

FOREWORD

Exquisite and powerful, fragile yet tough, there is poignancy and prayer in these poems and the spirituality is without piety. Jenny Johnson's Jewish ancestry forges through to a global spirituality which is inclusive. She paints pictures with her words and composes music too; her poems leave us with an echo in the mind and that mysterious sense of *déjà vu:* 'Suddenly, a child leaps high by the fringes of the water. / I dance alongside: I become White Wave.... / Always, we are close to an unseen guardian, she and I: / in the sorrow-joy; the sea-sky.'

Christine Michael

ACKNOWLEDGEMENTS

Some of these poems have appeared in the following publications: *Odyssey, Ore, Poetry Nottingham, The Poet's Voice* and *Summoning the Sea* (A Literary Festschrift for James Hogg).

For Marilyn

NEPTUNE'S DAUGHTERS

LETTING GO

Travelling north and east
from coast to centre,
I notice the Magritte picture
in a wing mirror:
my head against fine cirrus.

At the fringes of each county -
Cornwall, Devon, Avon -
I hear myself calling out
'Goodbye ... goodbye ...'

I remember that midnight clarity,
for taking leave of
birthdays; Christmas Days.

An ancestor - a refugee -
whispers in my hair.

REFUGE

In the unit for psychotics,
I am constantly shrunk by the eyes:
eyes like those of the punitive child;
the insecure parent.

The nurse allots palliatives; promises:
she walks with me everywhere.
But in the corridor - I fancy she has caught my malaise:
she hesitates in doorways. Till I lose her....

Acquiring a squat car from the outside square,
I drive without licence - towards the inner city:
towards buses - their foreheads too wide, too narrow.
I am frightened by the ones with fanlight eyelids.

Out of intense nowhere - the nurse appears; takes over:
I steel myself to feel safer.
But resident fear prevents both control and release:
and I lose her again....

After my collision with nothingness, I find myself
standing on the threshold of a huge, rectangular room.
The nurse has not returned.
What do I do? Enter - or leave?

Focusing, focusing on the wall in front, I recognise -
amongst a diagonal of paper hangings -
a handmade pocket of childhood:
I go inside ...

feel black and white feathers of the kittiwake, the
                                        guillemot:
feel west winds of the North Atlantic
mending my mind, expanding past, present and future
into one; and one; and one.

LIFE REVIEW

A mother attempts to videophone her son:
because of one half-broken button,
nothing is to be seen.
However - fancying she hears the
whispering of companions - she tries again.

All of a sudden - visions begin:
in the first - the schoolboy of nine crouches in front of a
stage hearth: others in the class, it seems, are chosen for
drama-without-scars.
Mother, like son, is the unobserved observer.

In her vision of the six-year-old boy by the sea -
toying with a watch that she has given him - she catches
                                    herself
stealing it back; and passing it on....
Recalling that north-east wind at the end of August,
she learns about his sense of unreality.

In a third vision - he turns into the baby in the grass:
becomes the imago; the six-pointed star....
When he jumps his wordless patterns into unlimited air,
she feels how he concentrates the wisdom
here and there; here and there.

At last, the videophone reveals him fully nineteen -
rejection pressed into withdrawn pupils:
beyond them - are signs of a dying star....
Finding its pulse - the mother begins to listen:
to respond in time.

OSCILLATION

Once, out of a silence at the centre of turmoil,
came feelings of being propelled between walls
that were dark sepia - not black.

At the ending of this chrysalis, she discerned a
subterranean market; and a man, expectant without

                                        gesture -
his eyelids closed.

Yet, despite the artificial light, she kept her own senses
fully open: she noticed the clover-and-gold rose - its
pippin-pure scent: noticed the escalator....

Till she was drawn towards sun; towards an afternoon of
roses and orchards: and Lindsay on a rope swing
turbulently colouring the air....

Learning to accept such movement,
she watched the child land on lichened grass -
curious; and unafraid.

SHADOW PLAY

Afraid no more of the roaring in her head -
of semi-paralysis, semi-fast eyelids -
she wills herself to come cleanly from the flesh:
and cannot achieve it.

The large painting ahead, opposite her bed,
shrinks to knee-size; is fixed to her quilt:
she finds such insistent absurdity
threatening as a wasp.

In the next breath - she is looking into her
fig-brown eye; is trying to touch her
pear-moist cheek: she feels so close to herself -
yet remains too distant.

It is Advent dark in the waking-world: here,
there are tones between moon and sun.
Of its own accord, the bed shifts backward:
is pulled towards an invisible door....

In the waking-world - she immediately thinks of
Chirico; Magritte: of the breaking and the building:
the balance: the release.

ART DECO, MIAMI BEACH

The New Year translucency remains within sea:
art deco turquoise.
The sky looks full of itself, with its
frequent metallic fowl.
Underneath it, young men lounge on chaises longues -
salt-clean; keen for uniformity.
Everywhere, there are pastels of purple, coral, jade.

The foreignness of Florida is stronger than that of
Italy, Germany: the language of English conceals
parallel rather than linked worlds.
People have an air of detachment:
a vocabulary of charm.

As I walk along the pearly beach,
my mood shifts: I begin depressed by the
absence of cliffs - of vitality in
tides and condominiums.
The rhythm in my hip - the afternoon light
laced with a wakening wind - pull me to the pier:
to the pelican's poised beak and wing.

In a while - willing to connect - I focus on detail:
the Beth Jacob Synagogue; the Wolfsonian Museum.
As six o'clock darkness falls, ocean-front hotels
line their aprons with premature loudness.
Puerto Ricans, Cubans, have opened bikini-thin shops.
At South Pointe, by a fitness circuit,
the elderly, orthodox Jews whisper.

The art of imitation - imitation of art? -
is as constant as in ancient Rome.
Americans pay homage to it in limousines -
or on roller-skates.

BREAKING FREE

Wherever she treads on those fringes of town
that encompasses her fear - there, it comes upon her;
and there: a mean, green shed;
gray-roofed; opaque-windowed;
its doors semi-ajar - like trappers' arms.

Then, it is in her backyard: hard by the
washing-line, the play-square, the kitchen.
And then, it becomes the bedroom:
the narrowing, gray-green walls
pinching the dregs of childhood.

Whenever she hears his drunken steps on the stair,
she pretends to hide beneath blind blanket;
to cover her eyes with stiffening hands.
She attempts to scream at her lock-less door -
but the larynx goes cold....

Sick Mother lives on pilules and elixirs;
is enclosed in a world of sorrows kept hot;
of simmering denial.
Such helplessness binds her daughter as fast as
Father's abuse. Night after night, she etches
'Liar! Guilty!' on the bruised heart....

Just once, looking in the glass, the girl acknowledges her
pair of wigs - blond basins trapping her
spring of hair: which she imagines
long as a wand, full as a curtain;
free ...
freer than a mountain wind.

REUNION

Here comes my teacher of Latin and drama:
she walks on-stage in a gold toga.
As willing audience - as designer - the whole of me
cries out for silver on indigo:
Ursa Major, the full moon....
To complement Rome, however, she adopts the role of
English priest: she asks for a pot of
frankincense, not silver.

Old girls, we risk linking past hearts -
dancing our goodbyes in the school hallway.
Even as we look at her, she is rising to the
height we remember: yet her hair begins changing
from auburn to gray....
The paradox cannot be grasped: we let her go.

On returning home, I discover a doll's house
with its front removed. The dolls are elderly:
my mother, my godmother, my mother's best friend.
All the compartments are fully absorbed by
diligent nurture: I cannot participate ...

except in the one space - which is half reserved
for the wardrobe mistress.
I give her my night-blue coat with its threadbare lapels.
She will adapt it: will embroider it with
many constellations; whole moons.

PERDITA

Although I have entered the ancient heart of a wood -
and have circled it for hours -
I cannot find a source for
this crying of a baby:
this crying without crescendo; without rest.

Suddenly, a lake's broad face peeps through the firs;
and a white swan floats towards me,
looking me in the eye:
she climbs on to the bank as if to make for the
lakeside well. Thirstily, I follow.

Willing the water to rub from awareness
my nightmare of tears, I find myself
staring through refectory windows: staring past
meals at the hearth; right into the far, far corner -
into the howls of an old baby.

Instantly, as I become her,
I am sucked into the loud light, the pattern of
pain without centre....
Then, half separate, I stand at the refectory door -
and walk towards her; and take her to the
cradle of myself: to the room's hearth:
the cauldron, the ladle.

TURNING IN

I found myself in a sea-healer's house:
her son's clay homunculus lay on the table -
crippled; waiting for completion.
The boy was allowed to come and go....

As I travelled inland - clay sorrows
lodged in my throat: turned
to a burn of tears on sea-cleansed cheeks.

At home, in the dried dark, I discovered a
blonde usurper in my fireside bed:
I ordered her to leave; but she refused.
'There is always room in the priest's house,' she
                                                    snapped.

Wandering from dust to dust - staring in
midnight mirrors - I watched an unfamiliar ghost
pass through dilapidated walls.

In a neighbouring space, the unknown, silent lover
cowered - afraid of her own shadow.
I embraced and kissed her: she enclosed herself
much more than the ghost; or the usurper.

The finest of priests was a sea-healer -
the one whose son was allowed to come and go....
As soon as it was daylight, I would return to her house.

BORDERLAND

Ascending towards midsummer,
with evening clouds over the river Otter -
over the curve of incoming tides -
I am drawn to the border of newborn consciousness.

These wildfowl are stilled: they are held within
                              reflections of
taming sunlight. High on my right,
a helix of larksong begins....
Whichever way I turn, there are mellowing headlands.

In Sidmouth, I am nourished by straight rain;
by the cerise-browns of Devon sandstone.
Challenged further west, I run along the damp shore
in luminous boots.

The estuary beach feels abandoned
except for the gull and the shell -
and a current of expectancy
out there ... in here.

But now, where do I go?...
The essence of the place calls out: 'Today, you have
                              sampled:
tomorrow, you travel inland:
here, on the very edge, you may play ... play.'

Suddenly, a child leaps high by the fringes of the water.
I dance alongside: I become White Wave....
Always, we are close to an unseen guardian, she and I:
in the sorrow-joy; the sea-sky.

MANY: ONE

When a street-performer rests against a stone wall -
and I touch her waist, her tapioca hair -
she remains unmoved.
Later, I observe her bending over a balustrade -
intensely continuing to talk, talk; to make brighter
                                            scenes.

Indoors, amongst the film's many extras, I detect
Daisy, tanned, waving her hand at my
cleansed face - at my curls tied back
like an ancient Sunday child's.
She greets me - but not as I am.

It seems I am led along tapered corridors,
and punctually brought to the attention of a nun -
who insists that we have an appointment;
but I, losing contact with the geography of time,
know nothing of this.

When I try to purify the details in her
scrubbed white basin - I notice a trapped scorpion
swimming the core of its frenzy round and round:
and I lift it out. But the shade of a thin man
steps in - and flattens it.

At once, I am slipped from one moist border to another;
am taken on wave after wave of expansion ...
contraction:
till scorpion, nun, performer, Daisy, become many
                                            more ...
become one.

NEPTUNE'S DAUGHTERS

Dreamwalking on to the campus of my heart,
I am lost.
The heart cannot be honed like thought:
lessons to be learned are without timetables, indices.

Outside the iced wall that Neptune saltily eats,
the small town sells many maps, many clocks;
and I find my level way to the boundary
between town's end and sea's tumultuous start.

An ageless longboat - without sails, without oars -
is tossed to untimely dying by twilight's violets and
                                        grays.
A second boat, alive with oarswomen,
glides into sudden sight by harbour walls....

My sister from over the water -
you have opened doors in a number of walls:
now, look into my campus-heart;
into my hushed brightness.

EVEN NOW

Even now - in my forty-ninth year -
I am still without appropriate fear
of the lion rampant.

I do not admire him either -
but am resigned, like my ancestors were:
like a marked Holocaust Jew.

Again and again, the lion has mauled my soul:
again and again, I seek a position where I may
take in the slow, dark balm of the mothering sea.

Inland, I find the baby who is innocent and wise;
yet wherever I stand, I cannot see who holds her;
and who becomes the giver - and who the receiver.

Even now - full forty-nine years after the Holocaust -
I do not require a fatherland....
Where is the mother?... Where is the sea?

NOVEMBER 2ND

All Souls' Day: day of my birth.
Alone, I come to the asylum-hotel.
Belonging to all time here, I stand in the foyer,
and glimpse from the edge of my vision
the admission of a young man -
his chaos controlled by tranquillising giants,
and behind dark glasses.

Climbing a number of flights of
hastily narrowing, spiralling stairs,
I arrive at where a white-clothed proprietress
pauses - matronly in her smile:
in her denial of dislocation - of the door
locked and bolted; the opaque window.
A nurse lingers - out of her view.

Descending the back stairs,
I find myself in a tunnel, barely lit -
its walls and ceiling unplastered, revealing
the unique fragrance of psychosis....
Along this forbidden corridor, shrivelled creatures
mutter and shuffle. I cannot communicate:
I observe.

Before my throat tightens - even before I have
spoken your name - you are coming towards me,
sister of my soul: your fairness seems an illumination....
One by one, all subterranean guests are
moved by your stillness: you unlock them; unbolt their
doors.
Male and female, they follow us patiently -
climbing that straight, wide staircase

to the nucleus of the house: a landing facing east
where an arched, stained glass window admits
a whole birthday of light through its red, gold and blue -
engendering presents of energy, clarity,
communication....
You have asked for the woman in white to join us:
we form an expectant crescent. From clearest sky,
sunlight taps, taps the brightly stained.

OUT OF SEASON

There are many guests in my parents' house.
When I return - all prodigal daughter -
it is Alice who stands in the hall:
her hair is the colour of rust; thin as a
rag doll's.
She is tired; and unprepared.
'Would you mind *not* calling me Mother?' she pleads.

In most of the rooms - uppermost, lowest - there exists
the feel of school, the diligence of pupils:
any fear, any anger, is unexpressed here;
every void in every woman is continuously filled, and
                                    filled.

'Where is the compartment for my luggage;
for my rage; ablution; sleep?'
When I inquire in a whisper -
no one gives me an answer.
And when I begin my crying out -
no one stops smiling....
I am tired; and unprepared.

PLAYROOM

Allowing herself to enter fully into her memory,
she found she was standing in a childhood bedroom:
found manifestations of adulthood -
garments, accoutrements -
side by side with decorative shelving of
rhymes, fables.

Gradually, she noticed the doll, the tricycle:
how topaz button eyes began to challenge hers;
how lacquered toes manoeuvred pedals -
till a shift was willed from wine carpet road
to pink linoleum pavement.

One by one, clocks of all ages took time
to divert her attention:
the first remained silent in its slate-blue coat;
the second chimed inappropriate hours
that applied to either future or past;
the third, more modern, was plainly precise.

The woman - before she could cry, or smile -
knew she would give her hands to winding, regulating,
arranging, discarding.
This was the playroom of everytime, everymood:
as with the hands, so with the mind.

ALL HALLOWS

All Hallows light, brittle between highest, south clouds,
feels essence most when shell becomes fractured:
an essence which seems sucked in, seems blown out -
beyond any orbit.

Indoors - eyes clasp the clover-pink vaporiser;
in the shade, heart-shaped holes in its sides
provide lights for giants - patterns for the plain wall:

behind the scalloped circle of the main window,
candleflame constantly wavers ...

SECONDS

ILLUMINATION

In my vestibule of solitude, I meditate on light:
I remove every vestige of dread, of self-pity;
I move away the films of sloth, the cataracts of guilt.

As the dawn washes in, with its quantum of mercy,
safely to their graves go the faces of the night -
re-embalmed, and made benign.

ATONEMENT

How oddly they met!
The daughter who walked with a negligent step
and the parent who wept.

Unaware of each other's compulsions or fears,
they halted. Apart.
They gazed at the space where a home had once fallen,
saluted it slowly. Together.

Whatever had happened to hold them so still,
to release from each being the pain of estrangement
and let in the love?

THE HOSTEL

She coped very well between the chippy and the
synagogue -
coped in a hostel run by the quaintest of
leonine women: a place where the yellow had darkened
years ago; where breakfast and supper were kept in a
basement; where beds remained cold enough for floor-
mats
to become coverlets.

Though since there was always a knowing crowd of
hands
to negotiate for her, Sally could relax with her
permanent crutches, her faint vocal impediment.
An optimist in a sky-blue print, she careered towards her
factory punch cards in a matching three-wheeler ...

till the lioness retired; till the carpenter came, the
decorator;
and 'self-catering' was the term....
Painfully, girls moved out - the old camaraderie
grown thin as a walking-stick.
Scandinavian Christina stood daily at the window -
impatient for her fiancé.

Sally - to whom levels and weights were no longer
familiar - considered her return to the Lancashire town
where,
formerly, she had been ignored. She played a portion of
her
record - entitled, 'Arrival of the Queen of Sheba':
played it over and over; very loud.

BARRIERS

She stands in the allowance queue absorbed in her
                                        Kafka;
pregnant; unaccommodated.
Everything about her is conspicuously pallid:
the khaki coat; the sallow finger;
the anti-hysteria face.

In their nourished house,
her brigadier father and her satellite mother
are engrossed in so much guilt, so much self-pity
that they grow exhausted -
and forget to unbar the door.

The queue for benefits jerkily shifts.
The foetus - a future mediator perhaps -
turns without warning in his wet elastic habitat.
The girl ceases reading -
and is not unaware of involuntary softenings.

THE BRIDGE

A month or two after his fifty-first birthday,
James was taken to the bridge.

The therapist ordered her twenty-eight patients
to keep to the left; to walk in pairs, sedately;
to watch collectively the orange foliage.

James disobeyed: he stepped on to the opposing
footpath;
stopped before the advice for intending suicides.

Scared of neither depth nor height,
he stared at the decreasing obscurity of the river:

it was forty years since he had sensed this bridge,
since he had found on the other side his twin brother;
disinfected; one-eyed; unacceptably dead.

The therapist purposely failed to notice
his need to communicate, to comprehend,
but holding his institutionalised hand, led him blandly
away.

The unbiased westerly wind simply anaesthetised.

CHIROPODY

On the third Thursday of each month,
Alice boards the green bus:
her daughter Hilary makes for the upper deck.
They journey across the Downs to the Blackboy,
Whiteladies Road, the Victoria Rooms.

In the Clifton waiting-room, Hilary stares at the ceiling -
the cornices, the roses - while her mother, behind shining
doors, anticipates treatment. The chiropodist smiles
through strong lenses, his hair profuse on his forehead.

Later, they visit a house with home-made fruit-sweets
in the window. And on their return, Roland, the husband,
massages Alice's stockinged feet with uncomplicated
warm hands....
It is nineteen fifty....

Hilary watches, hypnotised. These feet are as pampered
as the dogs, the rich leather of each lace-up
shaped specially for deformity. Those shins are too thin
for that big-boned frame: the ankles are frequently
                                        sprained,
crêpe-bound. Occasionally - when weakened eyes
                                        misjudge
boiling water - a toe-joint, an instep, is gingerly
anointed with copper-and-gold.

ALBION STREET

Though once the main trading-zone of this maritime
town - nowadays it seems to be nothing but a brusque,
slender hill; with a February of buildings.

the focus - a place frequented even more than the pub,
the junk-shop, the ironmonger's - is a chippy: managed
                                        by one
with positive hands, and hair the colour of batter.
Her white tiling is immaculate.

A boy with doe's eyes hides there from school bullies:
he is attracted to the illuminated ochre; the controlling
                                        smell.

LINES

Counter to the mists of Maundy Thursday,
here, at last, were the cleaned colours of St Erth;
the uncrowded light.

Most of the way to Newcastle - the solicitor thought -
she would crochet: the motion increased her appetite.
In her rucksack were sandwiches of homemade
                                                mayonnaise,
cartons of garnet juice.

She did not mind confiding in a stranger - even in
one who compulsively questioned. Her eyes, under the
abundant, bouclé hair, glinted like rare
sweets. The meaning of her name - Moira - was
                                                'destiny'.

She had lived before - would live again, she promised.
Quite single in the extended family, she had waited
just long enough with her Cornish house, her four dogs:

now, she would throw a goodbye to her Newcastle
                                                mother,
and would turn from the practice of advice, analysis,
to the life of a travelling musician - classical guitarist.

... Some time later - the stranger exchanged his lines for
sandwiches, cartons.
Stepping on to the platform where they hoped for
                                                connections -
he sensed how his acquaintance began to diminish; and
                                                age.

LINKS HOUSE

Opposite the golf-links, your spring house is a precinct
                                                    for
skeins of a pearly rose light: everything
pulsates at a different, silken rate; is unfussily
netted.... Nothing is permanently dead.

You are the one who spins; who contains; who creates
all the interstices: who understands that calms of families
                                                    and
friends respond to each other.

A picture of your granddaughter Harriet sits in the
                                            alcove -
quite far back, like a deep-set eye - a challenge within
                                                    the
cheekbone; an infant infinity in the Highland blue of the
iris; her hand extending its gifts to the whole of the
                                            world.

You offer me yoghurt and grapes in scalloped dishes:
an astringent taste; an emollient texture. And I sense how
                                                    your
detachment, your tones of leaven, are involved.

HEAT

Too soon after the turbulent freak cold
of June, the heat yawns - instantaneously old.
At night - I am insomniac; youth will not co-operate;
a moth jumps frenetically from peak to peak
of the most suffocating quilt.

As I write by a weak darkness, as dust ceases to parch,
as a bulbous moon hangs in the stained east
above the insistent, gristly vibrato of a gull -
I expect those nouns to anoint, not scorch....
What shall I tell?... What will alleviate best?

ARSON
(November 3rd)

Moments after the lane's light has ceased,
negative thoughts are pitched through her living-room
                                                                    glass
in the guise of an outsize, Guy Fawkes rocket:
its premature explosion releases a legion of emotions.

As tangerine hunger trespasses on the inner silence,
anger joins forces with terror; threatens to
consume the marrow.

Yet towards dawn, a distancing begins;
at the same time, a strange euphoria becomes:
attention is given to the law, the brigade, the papers;
camera lenses, luminous hands.

Items that matter - her manuscripts, her piano -
simply wear that powdery mourning-garb:
they look positively unscarred.

Those fragments of fear, anger, joy, are
swept up by a revived consciousness that
fire - like water - is both creator and destroyer;
and that home - like belief - is at once a haven and a
                                                                    prison.

GLASTONBURY TOR

Christmas morning. They drive through the wet streets
from Greinton to Chalice Well. Here, cupping hands,
they taste moving water - and approach the stile on a
path populated by thorn-berries.

She climbs up the west face of the tor - conscious of a
strong sense of direction: if she pauses to glance
behind, a power swivels her round to the east - as it
turned her earlier, in Glastonbury Abbey.

The hurt of the breath is caused by more than the
unaccustomed Christmas altitude: there is the gravity of
                                                    fear
to overcome. She focuses on the tower - to which St
                                                 Michael,
archangel of this new age, lends his spirit.

Below - to the south - a hemisphere of mist is
illuminated by silver sun; to the north -
a rainbow manifests; in the west there are fast clouds -
in the east, the undertones of wildness.

Earth, air, fire and water! Inside the tower,
people link arms in a circle - chanting the Om,
listening to their didgeridoo-player. His mother
recites an invocation: they echo it, line by line.

Prayer for global healing spirals through the square
aperture above them: spirals towards the east on the
west wind. Huddling together, they are mindful of the
O - symbol of nothing; yet also of what is beyond
                                                 nothing.

MORTEHOE

On the north-west point of Devon, where sea may turn to an
ocean - a point famous for shipwrecks -
past the cliff cemetery, full of new graves,
I walk beside the moist midsummer grass, between
outcrops in gorse: until I can see, most shiny in the north,
Bull Point lighthouse - whitened against the noon cobalt,
the greened folds of water.

Far below, there are two beaches, the more distant one
near Woolacombe: both resemble wombs - the first
seemingly hostile, the second lined with sand....
I reach the first uterus by a steep path,
feeling at worst claustrophobic - the slate-blue,
angular nakedness of rocks offering nothing but the
reminder of carnage.

Clambering on to its mini-peaks-and-plateaux,
I become aware of subtler qualities - of
clover and gold strata: become familiar with a
brine-thrawn texture: attempt to recapture
an ecstasy linked to childhood holidays....
Between the shelly rocks, the tide
stretches its fingers: I shift to the womb of sand.

Watching the Atlantic - or searching in vain for the
recollected guest-house - I sense, at least,
an increasing need for the tactile; the experience of
self-birthing.

CALDEY ISLAND

South of Tenby, there rises an island of contrasts:
sculped out of a mountain limestone; out of an old red
                                           sandstone;
the one stratum tempering the other....
Springing from the depth of their meeting, is an
                                    abundant, fresh water.

Inside the priory - narthex, choir and sanctuary form
St Illtyd's church: warm asylum for the
inscribed Caldey Stone - the sandstone relic of
Celtic brotherhood.

The other church, St David's, has a painted
green interior: is more chaste.

Today's Cistercians make perfume and chocolate -
for tourists they seldom see.
How different from those kinder times of pre-war
                                   Benedictines;
from a sanctum of Celtic saints -
Gildas, Illtyd, David, Samson...!

Caldey: 'Island of the Fresh Water Spring'....
Now, towards the lighthouse, a knot of tourists
gradually listens - absorbing the heat,
the horizonless sea; as a skylark ascends -
soloist in mist.

NOW

To know with only the left brain - the analyst's tool -
is a foolish business: a knowledge walled in.
To know with the bone, the heart, the intuition,
is a matter beyond dimension.

Emotion, like weather, is an unremitting flux;
time and time again we are drawn, drawn into a vortex:
till we sense no more than the shadow of our future;
the duskiest of dreams.

Words are in memory of the present: become the
afterthoughts of paradox - constantly releasing and
concealing. 'Now' is a syllable yelled in the wind:
memorable.

Without the quiet knowledge of the centre -
whose present is not between past and future -
the pain of the vortex is unbearable; unplaceable.
Yet now - we are shown how to suffer; to bear: to be
                                                    borne.

SAPPHO

A PRAYER TO APHRODITE

Richly enthroned, undying Aphrodite -
bewitching daughter of Zeus; and honoured goddess -
I implore you, do not tighten my heart.

But come to me now.... In the past, hearing my
distant love-cry, you left the goldenness of your
father's home, and came

in your yoked chariot. Towards the darkened earth,
numerous, quivering sparrows carried you
swiftly, beautifully, through mid-air ...

and without delay, found me. And you who are favoured
asked me - with that timeless smile - what had happened.
Why did I invite you?

What was my strongest desire in the midst of this
                                          madness?
'Whom do you wish to entice?' you asked.
'Who is the one that wrongs you, Sappho?

Although she avoids you - soon, she will follow after
you;
though she refuses gifts - soon, she will offer them;
and though she withholds her love - soon, she will need
to respond.'

Come to me, even now, and release me from anxiety;
satisfy the intensity of my heart:
you yourself, be my ally.

TO A YOUNG GIRL

He seems like one of the gods -
that man you are facing:
who so closely attends to the fragrance within words;

to the light within your laughter....
It is that which confounds me:
each time I glance at you - I am without sound.

My tongue is locked; and at once, a fine fire
glistens beneath my skin. I turn blind; there is a
whirring in my ear.

I am awash with love - unable to be still....
Fainter than leaf's light,
I am drawn towards my dying.

THE STARS AND THE MOON

Once again, the stars encircling the fine moon
conceal their burnished contours: this is the time of
moon's wholeness - of intense radiance
permeating the earth.

THE EVENING STAR

Hesperus - who reunites all things dawn has dispersed -
you have nudged the goat; you are calling upon sheep;
you deliver the child to its mother.

PARTING

Undoubtedly, death is welcome....
Tearfully she left me - telling me over and over:

'Sappho, what sorrow we bear!
Unwillingness fills this going away.'

I replied: 'Leave peacefully, and remember me;
for you know I have nourished you.

Nevertheless - lest you forget - I would focus on the
sharing of our tenderness.

For by my side, you wore many wreaths in your hair -
of rose and violet, crocus and dill -

and around your delicate neck, many charms
of entwined flowers.

Often indeed, you embalmed my head
with the richest myrrh of queens.'